Specialising in fun, lively non-fiction picture books,
Mick Manning and Brita Granström have perfected their
unique approach to children's books over ten years.
Sharing the illustrations between them and mixing up words
and pictures in all sorts of inventive and delightful ways
they have won many prizes, including the Smarties Silver Award
and the English Association Award.

Mick and Brita are married with four young sons.
They spend their time between the north of England and
Brita's homeland of Sweden. When not working on books,
they like to draw, paint and go canoeing.

The other books in the Fly on the Wall series are *Roman Fort, Pharaoh's Egypt* and *Greek Hero.* Their books for younger readers include *Yuck!, Snap!* and *Dino-Dinners.*

For Janetta and Jude

Front endpaper
In 851 AD two young friends, Grim and Ylva, visit a Viking rune stone on the island of Gotland.

Back endpaper
In 882 AD Thora and Thorkel play hide-and-seek around Uggla's memorial stone in Yorkshire.

Title page (background) and back cover
An image from a rune stone showing the Viking hero Sigurd killing the dragon Fafnir.

Researched on location in Jorvik, Dublin, Northumberland and Scandinavia.

Archaeological consultant: Dr Richard Hall. Dr Hall directed the Viking dig in York and helped create the Jorvik Centre. He is Director of Archaeology at York Archaeological Trust.

Find out more about this book at www.mickandbrita.com

No living creatures were harmed in the making of this book.

First published in Great Britain in 2006 and in the USA in 2007 by
Frances Lincoln Children's Books, 4 Torriano Mews,
Torriano Avenue, London NW5 2RZ
www.franceslincoln.com

First paperback edition published in Great Britain in 2007

British Library Cataloguing in Publication Data available on request

ISBN 978-1-84507-637-5

Illustrated with mixed media

Set in Albertus MT

Printed in Singapore

9 8 7 6 5 4 3 2 1

VIKING LONGSHIP

MICK MANNING
BRITA GRANSTRÖM

Consultant: Dr Richard Hall,
York Archaeological Trust

CONTENTS

Who were the Vikings?

'Viking' was originally a name given to the sea-pirates from the Scandinavian countries of Denmark, Sweden and Norway. In 793 AD, Viking pirates raided the monastery at Lindisfarne. The Christian monks were the only people writing books in those days, and they were horrified. They described all Vikings as bloodthirsty barbarians, although Vikings were probably no more violent than the Saxons and other peoples of the age. At this time England was divided into many small kingdoms and their Anglo-Saxon kings fought one another for power. England was a Christian country, but the Saxons had once worshipped the same pagan gods as the Vikings.

As they became more organised Vikings grouped together, sailing and exploring further. Waves of Vikings colonised parts of England, Scotland, Ireland and Europe in the 9th, 10th and 11th centuries. Their major settlement in England was the town of Jorvik (York).

Other Vikings sailed east, settling in parts of Russia. They traded and raided as far south as the Byzantine Empire. Others migrated north, colonising Iceland and Greenland – some Vikings even went on to discover North America. So Vikings were much more than pirates – they were skilful boat-builders, sailors, explorers, traders, craftsmen, clever farmers and poets.

Meet the Vikings

Our story begins in 864, and follows the life of a beautiful 9th century Viking Longship and the Vikings who sailed in her. Let's look in on some of them and see how they lived their lives in those dangerous times...

Dragging a Dragon

Here comes a longship! Dragged overland between river and sea, this dragon belongs to a pirate – a Viking called Ragnar.

Look!

The thunder god is throwing his magic hammer!

Ragnar has named his ship The Sea Dragon.

A small Viking longship is light enough to drag overland. This sort of shortcut is called 'portage'.

The word 'Viking' probably comes from the word 'Vik' meaning inlet. It could be that they sailed from inlets or landed their boats there when raiding.

Portage meant that Vikings could carry their boat between seas and rivers for short distances.

Viking ships were shallow enough to sail up a river but strong enough to cross an ocean.

We know about Viking ships from carved picture stones and the remains of beautiful longships discovered in Scandinavia.

In 793, the English monastery of Lindisfarne was burned and all the valuables stolen. It was the first of many attacks across Britain, Ireland and Europe.

Silver and gold was usually hacked into chunks to share out among the crew. It was called 'hack silver'.

Slaves were the bottom level of society, bought and sold like animals. They could even be killed or sacrificed by their masters.

Silver decorations from the covers of church books have been found in Viking settlements. They had been made into jewellery!

Niord, the god of the sea, could give a safe voyage or a bad one! Vikings believed in a family of gods ruled by Odin, the 'All Father'.

An eagle-giant called Corpse Swallower was thought to live at the edge of the world. It was believed that storm winds were made by his wing beats!

A Viking's sea chest might contain tools, weapons, clothes for the long voyage and loot on the way home.

Vikings carried dried bread, fish and fruit with them on their voyages.

Shipyard

Two young Vikings, Grim and Uggla, buy the broken longship from Ragnar's widow. Keen for adventure, they repair the damage, carefully healing *The Sea Dragon*'s wounds with a ship builder's skill.

Fresh 'green' timber was best for boat-building as it was soft to cut and didn't split like dry, seasoned timber.

Oak, or sometimes pine, was used for the keel and planking. It took about 12 big trees to make one longship.

Tests on the timbers of one Danish longship show that it was built in Ireland.

Sails were made of wool, and ropes were made of hemp, walrus or seal hide. Glue was made from pine resin and fat.

Warrior Training

Working for Earl Halfdan is well paid! But swordsmanship and battle skills can't be taught overnight. Yet they must learn fast. The invasion of England is about to begin!

Uggla is a fierce warrior. He is teaching the new recruits how to make a shield wall...

The 3-point plan on joining the Great Army was:
1. Fight! 2. Get rich with the booty.
3. Become landowners.

Many recruits were farmers, craftsmen and merchants looking to start a new life.

A Viking's weapons included the battle-axe, sword, shield and spear.

A new sword was very expensive so many warriors made do with second-hand swords, traded or claimed after battle.

Vikings believed the gods would help them if they were offered gifts as sacrifices.

Thor fought evil giants with his magic hammer. Vikings wore pendants shaped like hammers for good luck.

Sacrifice

By the old oak, where the gods look down, Grim and Uggla make a sacrifice. In this wild place, open to the sky, they ask for Thor's strength, Odin's cunning and Frey's blessing.

The skins of sacrificed animals hang from the branches.

Odin's ravens, Hugin and Munin, tell him what goes on in the world.

Hilda splashes blood on the statues!

Thor has a magic hammer called Mjollnir.

The Viking gods live in a place called Asgard.

Frey
Lord of growing things, harvest and peace.

Odin
Father of the gods. Creator of the world!

Thor
Mighty son of Odin! The people's friend.

To country folk, Frey was the most important god. His sister, Freya, rode a chariot pulled by cats. Her followers used magic called *seid*.

Frigg, the wife of Odin, was the goddess of home and motherhood. She spun the clouds on her magic loom!

Different peoples lived in Britain at this time. They included Saxons, Angles, Britons, Picts and Scots.

King Edmund of East Anglia did a deal with the Vikings and gave them supplies and extra horses. But they still killed him a few years later!

Invasion

The Sea Dragon is one of many longships dragged up on the sandy shore, spilling out men, supplies, weapons and horses. Earl Halfdan climbs the wind-blown sand dunes, shouting a battle cry to his men.

"The Vikings are here!"

Grim

Odin's ravens

Halfdan is a wealthy earl.
He wears rich clothes, jewellery and furs.

England was divided into small squabbling kingdoms. They were no match for the Viking Great Army when it invaded in 865.

Earl Halfdan was one of many leaders of the Great Army. Others included Guthrum, Anund, Oscytel and Ivar 'the boneless'!

Vikings believed Odin's warrior-maidens called Valkyries carried dead warriors to Valhall which means 'hall of the slain'.

Vikings believed they died because Odin needed them to fight at the battle of Ragnarok against giants and monsters.

To keep the Vikings away, many Saxon kingdoms paid them large amounts of silver.

King Alfred's West Saxons fought back. Their victory in 878 made the Vikings agree to a treaty sharing England between them.

Jorvik (York) was the cosmopolitan capital of Viking England. People came from far and wide to trade.

Many Viking place names such as *thwaite* (clearing), *toft* (farm), *carr* (marsh), *gate* (road) and *by* (farm) show where they made their homes.

Viking Farm

Grim has put away his sword and shield.
Spade and plough are his weapons of war.
He fights with weeds! Battles against rocks!
Nowadays *The Sea Dragon* carries horn-headed warriors. Uggla's loading an army of goats!

Because these place names occur alongside Saxon ones, it shows that Vikings lived peacefully with the locals.

Viking children didn't go to school. They learned skills from their family and friends.

Viking women had more rights than women in many other countries. They could own land, divorce and inherit property.

An Irish Viking woman called Aud migrated with her family to Iceland. She was one of Iceland's most important settlers.

Viking Women

Ylva Ormsdottir is a clever woman. She runs the farm, decides what's to be done in the longhouse, barn, storeroom and henhouse – Ylva rules the roost!

People sleep on benches along the walls.

Ylva sings while she is baking.

Birka Bread:

200g (1¾ cups) flour. 100g (1 cup) oats. ½ tsp salt
½ tsp cumin. 50g (½ cup) butter. 50g (½ cup) honey
200ml (¾ cup) water.

1. Mix the dry ingredients together.
2. Rub in the soft butter until the mixture is crumbly.
3. Add honey and water
4. Mix to a dough.
5. Roll into a fat sausage.
6. Chill for 1 hour.
7. Slice into ½cm (¼in) slices.
8. Cook in a dry frying pan until golden.

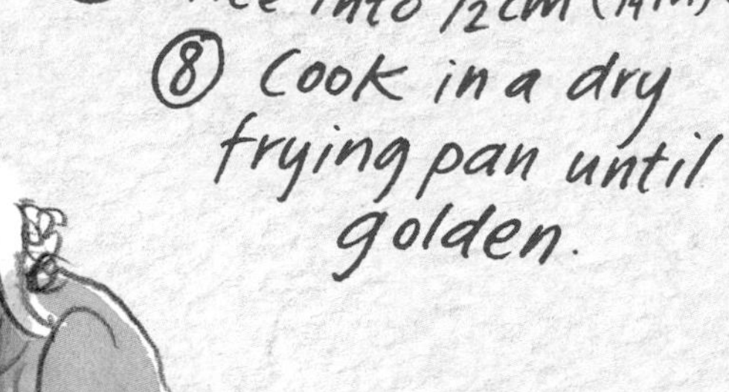

The hens wander indoors too!

Granny is ironing with a glass smoother on a whale bone 'ironing' board.

Women could be market traders, priestesses and farmers. One woman was a rune carver and Irish tales even tell of wild warrior women.

When the men were away raiding or trading, the women took charge of the farm and workers.

Jorvik

All along the smelly quayside, different ships bob at anchor. Grim takes a walk down Koppa Gata and buys a comb there for his nits! Ylva's bought a string of beads and some wooden toys.

Jorvik is a noisy, smoky place.

cupmaker

nobleman

weighing scales

wooden cups

baskets

antler and bone

Thorfast is a comb maker. He scratches runes on his combs: "Thorfast make a good comb!"

Viking buildings were usually made of wood, wattle and daub. They were roofed with straw, reeds or sometimes wooden tiles.

Leather shoes, cups, bowls, jewellery and combs were made and traded by the craftspeople in towns like York, Dublin in Ireland, and Birka in Sweden.

Vikings write with runes. This is the runic alphabet called **Futhark**.

ᚠᚢᚦᚬᚱᚴ ᚼᚾᛁᛅ ᛋᛏᛒᛘᛚᛦ

f u th a r k : h n i a s : t b m l R

Runes can be scratched or carved on skin, bone, wood or stone – the Vikings don't use paper.

Moneyers made coins by hammering a blank metal disc on to a metal 'die' that pressed a special design into it.

Everyone had nits (headlice) and fleas, and finds of Jorvik poo prove they were infested with tapeworms too. The drinking wells were too close to the toilets!

In one story, Frey is given a magic ship. In another, Odin murders a giant and then creates the world from its body parts!

Yule was a midwinter feast. There were 12 days of eating, drinking and worshipping. Today, it is still celebrated – but we call it Christmas!

Yule Feast

Grim hosts a Yule feast for friends and neighbours. His stories of Thor make the priest laugh out loud. Tales about Odin make everyone nervous – people glance over their shoulder when they hear about him.

Grim tells a story about the gods:

"I've stolen Thor's hammer," yells the giant Thrym. "If you want it back, let me marry goddess Freya!" Thor puts on Freya's dress, covers his beard with a veil and goes to the wedding. Thrym, thinking he's married Freya, wants a kiss. Thor snatches back his mighty hammer – "KISS THIS!" he shouts!

Every night the gods feasted on *Sahrimner*, a magic pig that came back to life each day.

Vikings used skis and bone-skates to hunt and play in wintertime. Feasts and festivals cheered up the cold months for everyone.

As years passed the Great Army split up. Some settled down in the north. Other groups fought on in the south or went raiding to Ireland and France.

By 917, the West Saxons once again ruled East Anglia and the Midlands but hadn't conquered Northumbria and its major settlement, Jorvik.

Raiders

Saxon raiders attack in the darkness. Smoking out Viking settlers like rats from a haystack. Grim and his followers grab rusty weapons. They break down the wall, escape in the smoke. Run to the river, down to their longship. Row for their lives while arrows rain down!

smoke in everyone's eyes

goats bleat

children cry

chickens cluck

dogs bark

They'll be back after the raiders have gone.

Luckily it's hard to aim arrows by moonlight.

They escape up the river where they have friends – but someone is missing.

The Anglo-Saxon Chronicle, a history book written at the time, records many big battles and small raids: Saxons v Danes, Danes v Norse-Irish and so on.

One page reads: "West Saxons went forth on the enemy's tracks, hewing them from behind with blades new sharpened."

Many Vikings hoped to go to Valhall, the hall of Odin. Others looked forward to Freya's hall, Sessrumnir, or Thrudheim, the hall of mighty Thor.

Legend tells that when killed by the trickery of Loki, Balder, darling of the gods, was pushed out to sea in a burning boat.

Vikings could be buried with bits of boats, in boat-shaped graves or even cremated. Their possessions, buried with them, tell us a lot about their lives.

Despite all the bloodshed and wars life went on. Anglo-Scandinavian farmers had to rebuild and begin again.

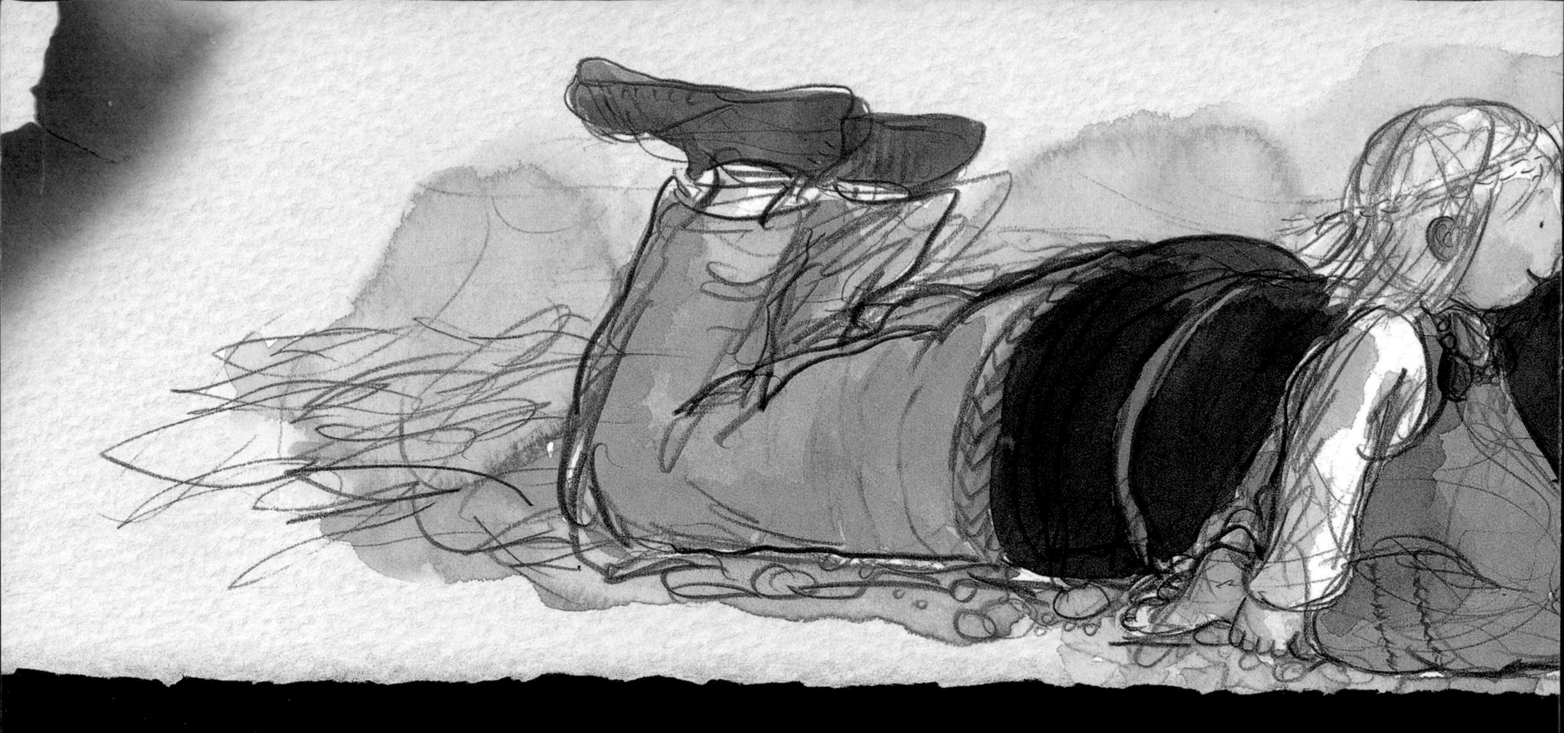

End of the Vikings

The Vikings conquered much of England, and parts of Scotland, Ireland and Wales. They traded and raided from these new bases.

When the Viking's Great Army invaded England in 865 AD, only the West Saxons led by King Alfred were not beaten. After many battles, a treaty was signed with Alfred, which recognised the Vikings' rule over the north and east of England. This area became known as the Danelaw. Viking leaders handed out land to their followers and many Vikings settled and became farmers, marrying with the local Saxons and Angles. Today, historians call these people Anglo-Scandinavians.

But for almost 200 years there were power struggles between the Saxons, the Anglo-Scandinavians, the Scots and the Irish Viking colonies. In 1016, Cnut the Great, a Christian Viking, became one of England's most famous kings by uniting Scandinavia and England and ruling wisely for many years. But when he died, his empire fell apart and the West Saxons once again became England's rulers. In 1066, King Harold and his Anglo-Scandinavian army beat off a Norwegian invasion, only to be beaten themselves a few weeks later at Hastings by William the Conqueror and his Norman knights. The Normans were themselves descendants of Vikings who had settled in France 150 years earlier – but that's another story!

What the Vikings left behind

Thousands of English words like 'egg', 'window', 'knife' and 'law' come from Viking languages. So do many greetings like 'hi' and 'hey' and surnames ending in 'son'.

Some days of the week are named after the Viking's pagan gods: Tyr's day, Wodin's (Odin's) day, Thor's day and Frey day.

Many Europeans (including European settlers who went to Australia and America) have Viking blood in their veins.

Remains of Viking objects, ships and settlements can be found in museums and visitors centres like York, Dublin, Roskilde in Denmark, Oslo in Norway, Birka in Sweden and L'Anse aux Meadows in Newfoundland – so why not explore the lives of Vikings and their longships yourself?

Glossary & Index

Anglo–Saxons (pg 6 and 33) The people living in England at the time of the Viking invasions included Saxons, Angles and Jutes. They were originally from Germany and Denmark and had themselves invaded England around 500 AD.

Anglo–Scandinavians (pg 35 and 36) What historians call the mixed population of Vikings and Anglo-Saxons living in the north and east of England from the 10th century.

Asgard (pg 19) Home of the Viking gods

Balder (pg 23 and 34) Son of Odin. God of beauty and light.

Britons (pg 20) Also known as Welsh and Celts. The people still living in Wales, and parts of southern Scotland at this time.

Byzantine Empire (pg 6) A huge wealthy empire centred around Greece and the eastern mediterranean countries.

Danes What the writers at the time called the Vikings of the Great Army who were mostly from Denmark. Some Viking settlers also came from Sweden and Norway, and fought in the wars.

Danelaw (pg 36) What the area of England settled by the Viking invaders eventually came to be called.

East Anglia (pg 20 and 32) A kingdom originally founded by the East Angles.

Frey (pg 19, 30 and 34) The nature god who made the earth fertile, and crops and babies grow.

Freya (pg 19 and 31) Goddess of fertility and magic, and the sister of Frey.

Frigg (pg 19) Goddess of motherhood and wife of Odin.

Futhark (pg 29) The Viking alphabet of runes.

Great Army (pg 7, 16, 21, 32 and 36) The organised alliance of Viking leaders and their warriors who invaded England in 865 AD.

Hemp (pg 15) A plant with strong fibres that can be twisted for rope-making.

Jorvik (pg 24, 28, 29 and 32) The major settlement of Viking England, now called York. Amazing archaeological discoveries can be seen at Jorvik Viking Centre and online at www.jorvik-viking-centre.co.uk

Koppa Gata (pg 28) The street of cup-makers. The original name for Coppergate, still a street in York to this day.

Knarr (pg 20) Cargo ships that carried supplies and settlers to Britain, Iceland and Greenland – and probably to North America, which the Vikings discovered and named Vinland.

Longhouse (pg 27) A Viking farmhouse.

Loki (pg 34) A trickster god with winged shoes. He eventually betrayed the gods, joining the forces of evil in a ship made of old fingernails called Naglfar.

Niord (pg 12) Father of Frey and Freya and a nature god of the sea and weather.

Normans (pg 36) The Normans were descendants of Vikings who had settled in Normandy, France.

Nits and fleas (pg 28 and 29) Blood-sucking insects living on the human body.

Norse (pg 33) Vikings from Norway who settled mostly in Ireland and Scotland, Cumbria and Merseyside.

Odin (pg 12, 19, 22, 30 and 31) Also called 'All Father' by the Vikings, Odin was the creator of the world – god of war and death as well as poetry and wisdom. Odin's wife is Frigg, goddess of motherhood.

Pagan (pg 30) A general name for people who were not Christians but worshipped nature and had more than one god.

Picts (pg 20) The people who lived in the north of Scotland at the time.

Portage (pg 8) Carrying a longship short distances overland.

Priestess (pg 7 and 27) Viking religion wasn't very organised but priestesses or 'Volva' used magic charms.

Ragnarok (pg 22) The final battle between the gods and the forces of evil led by Loki. Both sides and the entire world would be destroyed. But a new world would arise and Balder would return to rule it.

Seid (pg 19) Pronounced *say–the*, this is a sort of witchcraft practised by the priestesses who worshipped Freya.

Tapeworms (pg 29) These were very common in those days and were swallowed as eggs in dirty drinking water. They grow and live in the human body.

Thor (pg 19, 31 and 34) The most popular of the Viking gods. He fought evil with his magic hammer and righted wrongs. Many Vikings wore a hammer symbol round their neck for good luck.

Ugglebarnby (pg 24) A village in Yorkshire. It's named after a Viking called Uggleberd.

Valhall (pg 22 and 34) The hall of the dead where Viking warriors killed in battle went to party until it was time to fight at Ragnarok.

Valkyries (pg 22) Odin's warrior-maidens who carried slain warriors from the battlefield to Valhall. Thor's daughter, Thrud, was one of many Valkyrie.

Viking stories (pg 31) The Vikings told many exciting, scary, rude and funny stories about their gods. We know about many of them from a book called *The Edda*.

Wattle and daub (pg 28) Woven willow branches daubed with mud and dung.

MORE TITLES IN THE FLY ON THE WALL SERIES

Roman Fort

Patrol with a windswept centurion, eavesdrop
in the smelly toilets, visit a tasty Roman banquet,
listen to the crowd as gladiators fight –
you can even meet the Roman emperor!

ISBN 978-1-84507-124-0 (UK)
ISBN 978-1-84507-050-2 (US)

Pharaoh's Egypt

See how the mummy-makers perform their grisly work,
sail down the Nile with Huya the scribe, and creep into
the tombs with robbers as they steal jewels
by eerie torchlight.

ISBN 978-1-84507-100-4

Greek Hero

Follow Greek warrior Agathon on his way home
from battle, listen to Ariston tell tales of brave Odysseus,
learn Alpha to Omega with mischievous Hektor and hear
the crowd roar as you watch Olympic athletes sprint
for the finishing line.

ISBN 978-1-84507-683-2